D1520570

CHAPLAINCY: A HOSPITAL CHAPLAIN INTERN'S JOURNEY

APARA MAHAL SYLVESTER

TABLE OF CONTENTS

INTRODUCTION V

LOSING MY RELIGION 1

THE E.R. 5

MOMENTS OF GOD IN THE E.R. 9

MEETING GOD 11

INTRO TO A DIVINE PURPOSE 13

DIARY OF AN ON-CALL 17

THE PATH TO PRAYER 21

THE ELEPHANT IN THE ROOM 25

DEAR DIARY 29

WEARING HATS 31

NO REST FOR THE WEARY 35

FINDING MY VOICE 39

SILENT PRESENCE 43

GOD'S PLAN 47

DAY OF RECKONING 51

KINGDOM OF HEAVEN 55

AUTHOR'S NOTE

This book focuses on my personal journey as a Chaplain Intern. During my internship I encountered many private moments with patients and their families. I have mentioned some of these moments in my book. All identifying factors have been altered in order to protect privacy.

INTRODUCTION

From a young age I've always loved to write and never hesitated to put my thoughts and feelings on paper.

Many years ago, my father met an author and gave me one of her books. On the front page of the book is a picture of a cat. In a speech bubble coming out of the cat's mouth the author inscribed "Tell your stories, Apara!"

One day, I started to tell my stories.

I published my first book, a memoir, *Angel Child*, in 2015. *Angel Child* chronicles inspirational stories on how I overcame Mania. I have since published several children's books and freelance articles.

Just when I thought I had no more stories to tell, this book was born.

Chaplaincy: A Hospital Chaplain Intern's Journey documents my nine months as a Chaplain Intern in a large healthcare facility. This book is my personal story of how I entered into Chaplaincy and the experiences that followed from heartache to triumph. It is my personal account of the experiences I went through.

I invite you to now take my Chaplaincy journey with me.

Apara Mahal Sylvester

1 LOSING MY RELIGION

"That's me in the corner. That's me in the
spotlight, losing my religion." – R.E.M.

I'm not sure that you can lose something you never really had, but when I began this chapter the title popped into my head and seemed appropriate. It's a song by the group R.E.M. which was released in 1991, a year shy of when I graduated high school and when my formal religious education was completed.

I attended Catholic, or parochial, schools from kindergarten through to senior year in high school. However, I'm not a Catholic.

My heritage is Eastern European and East Indian. I grew up learning two monotheistic religions – Sikhism and Catholicism. Though not for religious reasons, I was sent to a

Catholic school, because the Catholic school system in my town was better than the public school system. I had religious education at home, but the bulk of my learning was in school.

In my heart I wanted to be a Catholic, I really did, until the time came when I didn't. It was during one religion class. I don't recall the exact grade this incident occurred, but it was one of the earlier ones. The topic of marriage came up and the teacher said if you weren't married in a church then you weren't going to go to Heaven.

I didn't question the teacher, but my stubborn mind refused to believe what she said. Because of their different religious backgrounds, my parents weren't married in a church. I knew my parents were good people, and I loved them dearly. I knew for a fact that they were going to Heaven. Right then and there my young mind knew that what the teacher said was pure hogwash.

I lost my religion that day. This was the precise moment when I stopped paying attention to what was being taught in religion class and when I stopped wanting to be a Catholic. Up to that point, I listened to and believed everything that the teachers said. Afterwards, I doubted everything they taught me, but I never, ever doubted that an all-loving God existed.

I believe in God, very strongly, but I won't go to church or any house of worship. I think organized religion is full of too many man-made rules. I don't like being preached at, and as God is supposed to be everywhere, why should I then confine him to one building on a Sunday morning?

Years ago, around 2005, I actually did go to church on a regular basis, and I enjoyed it. I loved the priest at this particular church, and this is why I went. He was unique. He had been married with children and after his wife died, he became a priest. This priest had lived life, he told it like it was, and I loved him for it. I do believe priests should be allowed to marry and have families. It would help them better preach at their services and keep it real like this priest did. This is just my opinion.

Ultimately, I believe in God and, to me, that's all what matters.

I'm just a speck, a tiny little speck of being in the Universe. I'm a small voice in the masses. But I know that there is an all-loving, all knowing God who hears me and listens, despite the fact I may not always agree with what his followers preach. For me, to have God's ear is enough. I do my best to be a good person and that's all I can ask for. That's all I believe God can ask of me, too.

In my Chaplain program, we occasionally had to write reflection papers. Below is my answer from one such paper which posed the question, *How do I speak theologically about why me?/Who am I to do this work?*

In answer to this question, I will pose another question; Why not me? I am a child of God and I am just as capable of shining God's light unto others as anyone else.

Some people are able to easily quote scriptures and Psalms. However, what resonates for me in this question is a line from the poem "Desiderata": "You are a child of the

Universe, no less than the trees and the stars; you have a right to be here." As a child of the Universe and a child of

God, I have an importance in this world, a place, and I feel called upon to do God's work of service to humanity as my duty.

2 THE EMERGENCY ROOM

During undergraduate and graduate schools, I worked in the Admitting and Emergency Room (E.R.) registration departments of a local hospital. Besides providing me with a source of income, I was always a people person and registration work allowed me to heavily interact with people.

I loved working in the hospital and this led me to pursue a Master's degree in Health Policy and Management. Though I chose this degree path, I was never really certain where it would lead me. I was young and I wasn't all too concerned about direction at that stage of my life.

I enjoyed my work, but I didn't know what type of career I could have in a hospital environment. I did my graduate internship in a lonely hospital office, and I didn't care for that too much. I was never good in math or science, so becoming a doctor or a nurse was out of the question. Back then, I only saw the doctors and nurses as the ones who interacted with people the most. I was never fortunate enough to have a mentor or guide, so I faltered.

Fate had other things in store for me. Right after graduate school, my life took a drastic turn when I got an opportunity to teach in Beijing, China for two years. From there I moved to Germany for two years before moving permanently back to the United States.

In the United States I held a few corporate jobs and had several periods of unemployment as well. I wanted direction but direction always seemed to escape me.

Fast forward to 2009. I was unemployed once again during an economic depression and desperate to find any sort of work, even part time. This was hard to do given my vast experiences and over qualifications. I then decided to revert back to what I knew from years ago: E.R. registration. One hospital I applied to did not require a resume, only a short description of my qualifications. So, I described my registration work and experiences from years ago. It took a year to be called in for an interview, but I ultimately got hired.

I never thought to compare it to a flashback, but in a way it was. Same as all those years ago, my job was to register patients. I went from bed to bed collecting personal and insurance data, inputting everything into the computer and having them sign the customary consent forms. I was just grateful to have a job and health benefits after a significant period of unemployment.

My position was an hourly, clerical position and a far cry from the corporate salary I used to earn. Some may have called this a step backward. I thought so too for a long while, until I fully embraced my role and realized that my life had come full circle. I had the chance to begin anew.

Little did I know, seven years later, I would once again have another new beginning.

APARA MAHAL SYLVESTER

3 MOMENTS OF GOD IN THE E.R.

I love working in the E.R. It gave me the opportunity to help people. Beyond my job responsibilities, I always went out of my way to get the patients blankets and pillows and anything else they needed to make their stay comfortable.

When I looked at the patients and their loved ones, I saw myself and my loved ones. Most importantly, I saw humans everywhere deserving comfort, dignity, and respect. Each time I was there I saw the faces of humanity.

Not everyone who comes in the E.R. will be healed. Death was a sad reality there. When the most critical patients came through the ambulance bay doors, I made sure to say a silent prayer of healing for them, especially the cardiac patients, as the heart is the most precious organ of all.

Once a man came in with cardiac arrest, loss of heart function. The paramedics handed me his driver's license so that I could enter his information into our system. I stared at his license picture for quite some time. He had gentle eyes and a kind face. I prayed for his health and recovery. I thought his life had been lost, but then I later learned that he was revived. I'm not saying I produced a miracle, but maybe my little prayer went a long way.

One night there was a lady with dementia screaming for her TV to be turned off. I went into her room and turned it off for her. She looked at me and said "Thank you. I love you." I looked back at her and said, "I love you too."

Another night a woman checked in for suicidal thoughts. When I was done checking her in, I touched her hand and told her everything was going to be okay.

One time a Spanish-speaking woman passed by my desk. She looked at me and affectionately said "Thank you, Mami." I had no idea who she was or why she was thanking me, but it brightened my day.

I experienced many "God" moments the years I spent working in the E.R. They were the beaming lights in normally hectic days.

I'm a believer in kind acts, and all I was doing was being kind and compassionate. Little did I know that, even before I knew what Chaplaincy was, I was doing Chaplaincy work without even realizing it.

4 MEETING GOD

The hospital I worked at was a Level I trauma center, which means there was round-the-clock in- house coverage by general surgeons and prompt availability of care in areas such as anesthesiology and critical care. Falls from a great height and car rollovers are just a few examples of what would constitute a patient being brought to a Level I trauma center as a trauma case.

When an incoming trauma was announced overhead, the "trauma team" sprang into action within only a few minutes notice. They quickly prepared one of the trauma rooms/bays for the patient. On standby were doctors, nurses, phlebotomists and x-ray technicians. Registrars were also considered part of the trauma team, as no testing could commence until we put the patient's name and date of birth into the computer to generate a patient ID number.

Whenever a trauma was called overhead, I was the first

person to volunteer as Registrar. I was a bit of an "adrenaline junkie" and liked the hustle and bustle and anticipation that occurred leading up to the trauma arriving in the E.R. Many times I waited out in the ambulance bay for the ambulance to arrive so that I could quickly get the information I needed and enter the patient into the computer system.

Everyone in the trauma team wore scrubs or a uniform, including myself. But there was always one lone man or woman who stood on the sidelines. They were dressed in business casual attire, small notebook in hand. Upon observing the scene, one could say that they stood out, but in fact they blended in and seemed to belong.

I became curious as to who these people were, so I asked. It was then I found out that they were Chaplains. I began to ask them about their role and what they did exactly. I learned that they provided emotional and spiritual support to patients and families. Chaplains were paged down to the E.R. when there was a trauma or other serious health event. If a family member was present, they spoke to them, comforted them, or just stood by them as a silent supportive presence. If no family was available, they would silently pray for the patient.

What I learned about what Chaplains do reminded me so much of my "Moments of God." I wanted to be like them. It was then I decided that I wanted to learn how to become one of them.

5 INTRO TO A DIVINE PURPOSE

Through my many conversations with different Chaplains, I learned that the hospital's Pastoral Care office had a Chaplain internship program called Clinical Pastoral Education (CPE). The program would allow a person to be a Chaplain intern, perform Chaplaincy work while at the same time learning about Chaplaincy. I was thrilled to learn of this program and eager to apply.

I "accosted" many Chaplains as questions kept popping up regarding Chaplaincy, CPE, and their own experiences. The Chaplains became my allies and my champions.

When I got the program application, I couldn't wait to fill it out. That graduate degree which didn't seem to amount to much would come in handy and become a blessing, my saving grace, as one of the program requirements was that you had to have a higher lever degree or be working towards one.

I later would learn that my reputation preceded me. Well before I submitted my application, everyone in the Pastoral Care department knew of the E.R. Registrar who was on a quest to become a Chaplain.

One of the application essay questions asked *What are your impressions of Clinical Pastoral Education?* This was my response to that question:

As an E.R. Registrar I am involved in the critical cases that come in, such as traumas, strokes, and cardiac arrests. In these situations, I come in contact with the Chaplains and see how they interact with the patient's family to help and comfort them. I imagine CPE to train Chaplains in how to help people in a variety of situations and aid in their spiritual and religious growth. CPE is not required of me, but I want to be in the CPE program. I would hope to learn from other Chaplains and Chaplain interns how to handle various situations in dealing with grief. I would like to become a Chaplain and CPE would assist me in achieving this goal.

In an email to a friend I excitedly announced that I had been accepted into the CPE program.

This is the email which I sent my friend:

I had thought about it so much and last September I finally put in an application. I was told they would be calling people in January, so I was waiting for 4.5 months before I got the call and subsequent acceptance. The program starts in September. There is lecture/discussion every Wednesday night from 4-8 p.m. I'll be required to do two 12-hour on calls a month which could be daytime or overnight. I will also have to spend five hours per week doing patient visits on an assigned floor. In total I will have to complete 300 clinical, lecture, and on-call hours. Luckily, I work part time so my work hours are flexible for the most part so that I can do this. I feel a calling to help people. I think I will be the right fit for Chaplain. I pray I will.

CPE is accredited through ACPE – Association for Clinical Pastoral Education – which is the standard for spiritual care and education. Upon completion of the program, I would earn one unit of CPE. Anyone wishing to become a Chaplain as a profession would need a Masters of Divinity degree or equivalent and a total of four CPE units, which would make them eligible to apply and be a board certified Chaplain.

In mid-September 2017 the CPE program commenced. There were 10 of us in my Chaplain cohort or group. I was not alone, though I did have the distinct advantage of having worked in the hospital for so many years and, mostly, knowing my way around it.

We met as a group for four hours every Wednesday for topic lecture and process work. The initial "didactics" or lectures covered the basics of Chaplaincy and what we were to do: What is Chaplaincy. Intro to CPE. On-call procedures. Patient visitation role plays. Prayer.

When it was time for my first on-call, I felt ready, even though I had no clue what ready was or what ready should feel like.

6 DIARY OF A FIRST ON-CALL

Tonight I am the one and only Chaplain for the whole hospital. Not only do I have a responsibility to the patients but also to God, acting as his vessel. I think I'm more nervous than excited. I just hope the right words and prayers come at the right time because for the next twelve hours it's just God and me here.

My first call of the night came just before 8:30 p.m. when the Chaplain I was relieving was still around, so we went to the call together. It was a stroke in the E.R. Medical staff was around the patient and family, so all we could do was stand by and offer up a silent prayer.

The next two calls I was on my own - both traumas in the E.R. The first call was for an intoxicated man who fell down 15 steps. His daughter was with him. I said a silent prayer for him then I kept the daughter abreast of what was going on with her father, me going back and forth to the nurse, all thanks to my many years of E.R. experience and observations.

The second trauma had no family present and was a self-inflicted gunshot wound to the face. I said an extra special silent prayer for help for him, for I felt he was a lost soul in need of more prayer.

ESS - emotional and spiritual support. This is what I write on my patient log sheet after every call. This is what we do for each patient and family, if present, even if it's only a silent prayer. We keep a patient log sheet and also an electronic log of the patients we encounter.

I thought I'd have a heart attack each time my pager went off, but I didn't; I just took it in stride. The pager doesn't shriek beep beep beep. It kind of plays a melody....do–be-do-be-do....so it's not jarring or jolting when it goes off.

When nothing is going on, and it could be hours of nothing, I spend my time in the on-call room. The on-call room has a desk and chair, phone, TV, and comfy bed. I pass the time watching TV and writing. Psychologically I'm not able to sleep knowing that at any minute my pager could go off. Also, sleep doesn't come easy with the way I caffeinate myself before my on-call with an extra-large coffee. You just can't sleep when you're "wired" from caffeine, fear, excitement, or a mix of all three. The most I can do is lie in bed with my eyes closed and just relax a bit.

It's quiet in my room except for the TV and I also hear the trains passing outside. As time goes by, I wish my pager would sound so that I could leave my little sanctuary and go help someone, even if only by silent prayer.

A few times I laid in bed and thought to myself, "I'm doing this. I'm actually doing this," almost in disbelief. I was so nervous about my first on-call until it actually happened.

It's now been over three hours since my last page and I'm actually wishing that another call would happen. I just took a walk to the vending machine to get my Snyders of Hanover Honey Mustard and Onion pretzel pieces fix. Also treated myself to some Sierra Mist from the soda machine in the common kitchen area of the on-call suite. One thing I can say is that the hospital does take care of those who have to spend the night here.

No chance of sleep or dreaming for me. It's now nearing 2 a.m. and I'm still feeling highly caffeinated from that XL coffee from so many hours ago.

Just after 2 a.m. my pager finally went off....another stoke in the E.R. I'm beginning to wonder if I'm ever going to go anywhere but the E.R. Eventually I'm sure I will, seems just not tonight. After this call, against my better judgment, I went to the cafeteria and caffeinated myself with a medium coffee, then back to the on-call suite for a Sierra Mist refill. Yum!

One of my fears of being a Chaplain is being able to quickly find my way around the hospital. Now, night one, I have only been to the E.R., which I know like the back of my hand.

Another fear I had was what do I do if I get three pages at

once; how to decide which page to go to first. Looks like that's not happening tonight. One night it will....just not tonight.

Going into this on-call I had many fears. Have my fears been dispelled? Somewhat, but I have not been challenged tonight. The test will come when I am challenged with a situation where I'll really have to think, speak, and pray on my feet and rely solely on God to guide me. I do pray now that, when this challenge comes, I'll be ready.

As I wrote this passage my pager went off - trauma alert in the E.R.,10 minutes. This time it was a fall of an elderly man. His son was present and visibly distraught. I tried to reassure him that his father was receiving the best of care. Otherwise, I remained silent. Sometimes silence is a form of comfort too. Of course, I silently prayed.

I thought 12 hours, and parts of my night felt like it was dragging, but now in the blink of an eye it's 6 a.m. Only 2.5 more hours to go. Seems like God's plan was to ease me into this new venture of mine.

It's now 8 a.m. On my way to the Pastoral Care office to meet my relief, when passing through the E.R. I saw the distraught son. I went into the room and asked how his father was. He was on a ventilator but stable. I told the son that I would say a prayer for his father. He smiled and said thank you.

That's what I can do. That's all I can do.

7 THE PATH TO PRAYER

I pray. A lot. Every night and often during the day.

As with my religious convictions, my beliefs on prayer are equally unconventional. In the end, they work for me, they are sincere and heartfelt, and I know my thoughts and intentions reach God's ears.

I don't pray to the Father, Son, and Holy Spirit as was taught in school. I pray to the higher power. I also pray to the angels, not God directly, because the angels are God's messengers and will tell God everything anyway. God is busy, so I utilize His messengers. This is how I rationalize my method of prayer in my mind.

I keep my nightly prayers simple because that's what I read in an excellent book called *Laws of the Spirit World* by Khorshed Bhavnagri. First, I give thanks for the blessings of the day. At night I ask for sleep because sleep is of the utmost importance. I ask to keep enemies away with the white light of protection. Then I state my intentions for the blessings I would like, such as on my family and my husband. I end my prayers with my own intentions, if I have any. Everyone else comes first and me last.

This is how my nightly prayer goes:

"Angels and high spirits, thank you for your blessings of this day. Grant me sleep, grant me rest, grant me peaceful dreams. Keep enemies at bay, grant me the white light of protection. Bless everyone in my soul family XYZ keep them safe, keep them healthy. Bless XYZ. Bless anyone in my life in need of prayer XYZ. For this I pray."

My husband prays and if he happens to be talking to me and I say it's prayer time, he'll stop. He respects my prayer time.

During the day my prayers are even shorter. I may simply say Angels and High Spirits grant me a good day at work, grant me a safe journey, etc.

Prayer came easy for me at home. It became a challenge for me during my hospital Chaplaincy work. I was able to "think on my feet" in many situations and yet I stumbled when it came time for spontaneous prayer. Silent prayer was easy, spontaneous not.

Some Chaplains offer up prayer during a patient encounter, but I rarely did due to my own shortcomings and lack of confidence in the area of prayer. Over time and with guidance, I became better at it.

Throughout my CPE program, we were required to write theological reflections papers. In one of my papers this was my formal personal assessment on prayer – describing my use of spontaneous prayer with patients.

Initially I was hesitant to pray with patients, because I was not good in spontaneous prayer. I also was unsure if patients wanted prayer. Over time I gathered a "toolkit" of prayers which I kept in my purse and used at appropriate times. I became more comfortable with offering prayer to patients. I don't think I will ever be good at spontaneous prayer, but overall I have become more comfortable in praying with patients. Spontaneous prayer is still something I need to work on.

APARA MAHAL SYLVESTER

8 THE ELEPHANT IN THE ROOM

I had a false impression that once I became a Chaplain, people would eagerly ask me all about what I did. That wasn't the case. Whenever I mentioned the word Chaplain in a social setting people usually quickly moved on to some other topic. It became easier for them to avoid rather than discuss.

Funeral Directors and Chaplains face the same stigma in their respective vocations – the perception of the Grim Reaper calling.

When I worked in the E.R., sometimes I would bring the Chaplain to a patient's family. As soon as I brought the Chaplain over and introduced him or her, I would immediately say that they would be their liaison to the medical staff. The introduction alleviated the fear that something tragic had happened to their family member.

Why is death and dying so taboo? We are all on this earth

for a very short time, and those who deal with the death and dying and provide comfort should be revered, not rebuffed.

When I wrote this passage, I had been a Chaplain intern at this point for just under three months. On this particular day I was at the hospital visiting patients on the cardiac and renal floors, as I do every Monday and sometimes Fridays. This day I was also Chaplain on call for 3.5 hours while the Pastoral Care staff enjoyed a staff outing, aka I was "holding the pager."

I received a page from a nurse on one of the intensive care units. I went up to the unit and met with the nurse. A patient's life support was going to be withdrawn and once that happened, he would pass quickly. The nurse told me the man had no family. She confided in me that she was religious and, for her, we had to do something for the man. As mentioned, spontaneous prayer was not one of my strong points, but I managed to ask God to give this man a smooth transition into his kingdom before saying the Lord's prayer. On my way out of the room the nurse thanked me for coming.

This encounter was meaningful for me. Never before have I been in a situation where just me and someone else were the only two people in the world who cared about a person, and I was the one called upon to pray. The power this holds is tremendous.

This beautiful story is one which I haven't really told anyone about, because it's the perfect example of the elephant in the room. No one wants to hear stories of death and dying.

I had another instance where a man had stage 4 lung

cancer and he asked me if I believed in the afterlife. We then had a discussion about heaven and reincarnation. Another elephant in the room.

Then there's the beauty, beyond death and dying. A new father paged me and asked me to say a blessing for his newborn to have safe travels home on a snowy day. I said a prayer for a long, safe, healthy, and blessed life.

To embrace death, something which I think many people don't understand or want to understand, is a calling for sure.

I take pride in what I do and cherish my role as Chaplain. What better gift to give people than prayer and comfort in unimaginably difficult times? It really is a gift. A gift that maybe Chaplains, Funeral Directors, and a select few others understand.

Chaplains take the elephant head on, and we embrace it. That's what makes us special.

Apara Mahal Sylvester

9 DEAR DIARY

I'm writing this on my third on-call, second overnight shift. So far, my night has been uneventful with no pages yet. However, the night is still young.

This on-call is different from my other two on-calls because so much had happened on previous on-calls. I've dealt with death, dying, strokes, and traumas. I'm by far not a pro at this, but the anticipation of what could be is no longer there.

Including tonight, I have been in the hospital 12 days straight, either from my registration job or Chaplain related work. The hospital is definitely a familiar place, but it's far from home. Lucky for me, when I come here, the longest I stay is 8.5 hours when I'm working, and the 12-hour on- call twice a month. Except for on-calls I'm here far less hours with Chaplain work.

One of my Chaplain peers described the overnight shift as lonely. I would venture to say I don't feel lonely, but I feel "solitude." It's nice to be in the on-call suite with just the TV and me, but sometimes I need to get out and see other people so I go take a walk to the E.R. As I don't really make friends at work, I don't have too many people with whom I can talk to, so I basically walk around, greet people then come back. I'm friendly, but I always believed in keeping work and personal separate.

Do I wish for a page? Absolutely, just something not too serious. A page would get me out of this room for a bit.

Tonight I'm thinking about God and what God thinks of me and what I'm doing, and I mean "What I'm doing" in a very broad sense. I'm a Chaplain doing God's work in trying to help and comfort people to the best of my abilities.

10 WEARING HATS

In the literal sense, I love wearing hats. Hats make me stand
out in the crowd and look distinguished. In the figurative
sense, I'm not so sure how I feel about hats.

When I became a Chaplain intern, I knew that I would be
wearing two hats in the hospital, Chaplain and Registrar. Out
of the two, I often wondered which one was the more
authentic me. I came to the conclusion that it was when I was
in my registration role. I was more "me." I could get stressed
and frustrated. I was able to curse, under my breath of course.
When I put my Chaplain hat on, these emotions have to be
suppressed. I have to be the cool, calm, and collected one.
Oddly enough, I could never escape my Chaplain role in my
registration hat. I get called Chaplain a lot by my registration
and other colleagues.

With my Registrar job and Chaplain intern responsibilities,

there were times I was in the hospital for days on end, some-times even two weeks in a row before I had a true day off.

When you work for a big hospital E.R., especially for so many years as I did, and you're there all the time, it's inevitable that you will run into the same people again.

When I became a Chaplain Intern, my biggest fear was that someone I had been Chaplain to would see me as my "registration self." One day, the unavoidable happened. I registered a man whose wife was at his bedside. She recog-nized me as being her Chaplain several weeks prior. It took a moment for the recollection to hit me that I had been the Chaplain on call and was in the ER with her and her mother when her father had passed.

It was awkward for me, extremely uncomfortable, and I felt inside that somehow my role of Chaplain was invalidated by this woman seeing me in work clothes. Ordinary and not divine.

I had a supervisor during my Chaplain internship who met with me every two weeks and acted like a mentor and guide. I told my Chaplain supervisor that I feel like Clark Kent and Superman. She asked me to elaborate and "tell me more." Tell me more was what my supervisor used to say when she wanted me to probe into myself a bit deeper.

Clark Kent is the "ordinary Joe," while Superman is the revered one. That's how I feel wearing my Chaplain "hat"--revered. When I'm not Chaplain--ordinary.

Could I have an identity crisis on my hands? It wouldn't be the first time this has happened to me. When I was younger

I floated in between two worlds--Indian and American--and struggled with it. I didn't feel as if I could be both nationalities all rolled into one, but I couldn't separate myself either. It was easier when I got older because I could morph into whomever I wanted to be. As an adult I wear this one elaborate hat, encompassing both my Indian and Eastern European heritages.

Why can't I do the same with my role as Chaplain and registration? Wear one all-encompassing hat? The roles are so different. Registration work has a business agenda. Chaplaincy work can have no agenda.

I don't have the answer to this. Maybe this is something I have to discover within myself.

Hats are about emotion. It is all about how it makes you feel. I don't know how I feel about hats, but I know I can't avoid them. I know I have to embrace them, but I'm not sure how. Maybe one day I'll find just one all-encompassing hat for everything, and I won't have to worry about juggling anymore.

APARA MAHAL SYLVESTER

11 NO REST FOR THE WEARY

Laughter does wonders to ease the soul. You have to have humor if you want to be a Chaplain. It's an important part of "self-care." Caring for yourself and ensuring that your mind and body get the rest and relaxation they need to rejuvenate. No one can function on an empty vessel.

Writing, for me, is a form of self-care. I find writing and words to be therapeutic and relaxing. Writing takes my mind off of everything.

This is another on-call dairy account of mine, a humorous one, about my ever-evasive sleep dilemma.

I've mentioned that sleep doesn't come easily to me, and at the hospital, impossible. Our on-call suite has a very comfortable bed. My peers that have done the overnight have told me they've brought their own blanket, pillow and even pajamas when they've been on call. I just can't do that. I don't want to come to the hospital as if I'm moving in. Too much work.

When I come to the hospital for my on-call, I bring my handbag along with a medium tote bag with my snacks, pens, and paper. That's it. On my way to the hospital, without fail, a stop at a coffee shop for the XL cup of pure bliss.

I had one overnight when absolutely nothing was going on. That night I decided to "try" and sleep. The first roadblock to rest was that I couldn't get undressed because the on-call suite was freezing cold, so I laid down on the bed fully dressed. I was wearing a dress and matching blazer and I kept worrying about my clothes getting wrinkled, so I tried not to move around much. I had to lay still like a mummy. Problem number one.

My hair and makeup quickly became problem number two. Easily solved. In ancient Japan the Geisha women would keep their hairstyles in place by raising their head off the ground on a special platform pillow called a takamakura, which prevented their hair and makeup from getting messed up. I made a "Japanese pillow" of sorts by folding up my pillow at the base of my neck so that neither my hair nor my makeup would get disturbed. If you've never tried this before I really don't recommend it. It's very uncomfortable.

Problem number three was the fear of actually falling asleep. I didn't worry so much about what if the pager went off; I worried about how I would react if the pager went off. I didn't want to be groggy and out of sorts having to quickly go to a call.

Amid all of these problems I don't know if I actually dozed off for a bit. I had a time lapse where I shut the lights off at around 1a.m. and before I knew it, it was almost 3 a.m., so something happened.

Just after 3 a.m. I got up, composed myself, and went to the cafeteria to get some food and coffee (yes, more coffee). While in the cafeteria my pager went off. Case in point, and I was prepared. I ended up going to a cardiac arrest where the patient expired. I was fresh, awake, and alert.

Why can't it be as easy as when I'm home? At home I just put on my comfy leopard print pajamas, say my prayers, and drift off to dreamland. In order to prepare myself for the overnight at the hospital I sleep during the daytime from about 11 a.m. to 5 p.m. That does actually give me adequate rest.

No rest for the weary aside, I love what I do. I don't mind doing the overnights, even if it means no rest. Once I go home, I fall into a deep and restful sleep. That's enough for me.

Apara Mahal Sylvester

12 FINDING MY VOICE

There are some encounters which, as a Chaplain, are momen-
tous and you just don't forget. The next few passages describe
one such encounter for me, one where I embraced my role
fully and the realization came to me: I'm a Chaplain.

Grief, for me, is the hardest to acknowledge. I almost
never know what to say to someone in bereavement situations.
I forget why, but in Chaplain seminar we're advised not to say
I'm sorry, probably because "I'm sorry" really doesn't mean
anything and it can be distancing. I tend to say "My deepest
condolences are with you" but beyond that, when someone
passes the words are hard to find.

Once I attended a code blue (cardiac arrest). Three family
members were present in the ICU waiting room. One woman
was crying deeply. I introduced myself, asked if they needed
anything, and one family member politely said thank you for
coming. At that moment I felt like a pastoral failure because I

wasn't needed and was politely dismissed. I didn't know what more to say, and I didn't feel comfortable to just be present only in silence. I felt useless.

Shortly thereafter, when the family member passed, I was paged back up to the unit. I escorted the family to the patient's room. The one who had been crying deeply, the woman's great-granddaughter, took off running down the hallway. I instinctively followed her. When she stopped, all of a sudden I found all the right words at the right moment:

Me: She was your favorite, wasn't she?

Her: (nodding) I wouldn't be here if it wasn't for her.

Me: How so?

Her: She did everything for me.

Me: Do you want to go to the room?

Her: Yes.

Me: Do you want me to come into the room with you?

Her: Yes.

When we got back to the room, I offered a bereavement

prayer, which the family accepted, and we also spoke a bit about the life of the patient before I left.

We learn a lot in Chaplain seminar about asking probing questions, making it all about the patient. I could have asked the great-granddaughter more about what her great-grandmother did for her in her life, but I didn't want to detain her from going into the room to see her. When I had been in the waiting room with the family, when they knew what was to come, what more could I have said? I did my best to comfort and be present. In the end, that's what a Chaplain is supposed do.

I came into my own and found my "pastoral authority" in that encounter. I walked away with a sense of knowing that I did exactly what I was supposed to have done.

All those years ago in religion class, I lost my voice. This night, I found it.

APARA MAHAL SYLVESTER

13 SILENT PRESENCE

"The test will come when I am challenged with a situation where I'll really have to think, speak and pray on my feet and rely solely on God to guide me. I do pray now that when this challenge comes, I'll be ready."

That challenge came in early winter. It was the worst case imaginable.

A young teenage girl had a fight with her mother. She drove off in a car. She crashed into a tree full impact. She was put on life support once she arrived at the hospital.

I was called to the pediatric ICU at the request of the patient's mother. When I got to the room the mother didn't say anything to me. Her head was down on the bed in her daughter's lap. I gravitated towards a corner of the room. I stood invisibly in that corner of the room and prayed silently watching the mother and daughter. The girl's two sisters arrived at some point and all were grieving at the bedside. I watched as they took turns kneeling at the girl's bedside, stroking her hair, holding her hands, laying their heads in her lap.

I was present in their grief, and that was all I could do. The entire time I stood in that corner of the room wanting the walls to swallow me up. I was utterly helpless as I watched a family's worst nightmare unfold before my very eyes. The room was eerily silent except for the puffs of the respirator keeping her body alive.

There was nothing I could do. There was nothing God could do because she was already in his arms. All that I could do was call upon God to give her soul peace and her family comfort.

There's an empathetic term called "sitting in pain." That night I sat in this family's pain so deeply it was as if I was atop quicksand. My emotions were as sunken down as that of the family. I felt that I was a part of them.

I silently prayed in my little corner of their unimaginable world for what seemed like an eternity. I have no idea how long I was there in that corner just watching the pain and suffering unfold.

They were going to take the girl off of the respirator and all life-sustaining devices. I had jotted my notes down on paper which was around 4:40 a.m. I knew the girl could go at any time, but it also could take hours as per the nurse.

I was with the family approximately two hours. When I felt that there was no more I could do at that time, I excused myself and told the nurse to page if I was needed. I needed air and to clear my head.

I went to the cafeteria to get away and for a bit. Shortly after my pager sounded. It was the pediatric ICU. The girl had been removed from life support and it would be just a matter of time before she was gone.

I let the family be alone with the girl in the room while I stood outside the room by the nurse's mobile workstation where I was able to watch the monitors. I watched as her heart rate slowly dropped until there was nothing. I was present at the moment she died.

After the family said their final goodbyes to her, I walked with everyone to the elevators. As they were getting inside the girl's uncle said, "Thank you, Chaplain," and gave me a hug. The elevator doors closed. I was alone in that hallway. By this time, it was about 6:30 a.m.

I don't remember what I did after the family left, though. I know I was as broken as that family was. I absorbed their grief and became part of them during the time I was with them. As a Chaplain, sometimes it's hard to separate yourself from a situation, especially after being with someone for hours under such a tragic circumstance.

The girl died but I survived. To this day I still don't know how I did it, but I did.

I don't remember much about the rest of that night, or morning. Thankfully, I don't think there were any other pages. I couldn't wait until 8 a.m. when I would then give my night report to the Pastoral Care office. I mentioned the case very briefly, as all I wanted to do was go home.

My supervisor was in the office. I could have spoken with her to process my feelings, but at that point I was exhausted and numb and just wanted to be silent. I was depleted.

At the end of my shift I somehow made the drive home and crawled into bed. If I remember correctly, I was off for a few days afterwards. I made sure to rest fully and practice a lot of self-care.

In one of my CPE coursework papers the topic of death came up. This was my response to the question *Why do we die/What is death's purpose?*

I don't have an answer to this, but we are all temporary beings on this earth for reasons I cannot explain. Heaven is eternal, but earth is not. I think death's purpose is to remind us of the temporary nature and fragility of life and for us to appreciate all of God's gifts in life while we have the chance to do so.

Being around death and dying did make me appreciate all of God's gifts. When I got home that morning, I'm sure I gave my husband a hug and my two cats some extra strokes on their backs.

14 GOD'S PLAN

Chaplaincy, in the beginning, was obscure. Then, the more I got into it, the more it became an integral part of who I was and my identity.

I think I never knew who I really was until I started the Chaplain program. I didn't know what life was like being a Chaplain. Later, I didn't know how I ever lived without it. I loved it that much. It's who I was, who I became.

Discernment refers to figuring out what is next, what is best for you. Well, before The Chaplain program ended, I was thinking about what was next. I had this amazing, though sometimes tumultuous, experience that I just wasn't ready to let go of come graduation day.

Police Chaplaincy spoke to me. I knew some police offers on a friendly basis and my deceased father-in-law was Chief of Police in the town where I reside. Over the coming summer, I decided that I was going to take a two-day police Chaplain course. I didn't know where it may lead me, but it wouldn't hurt to have the certification.

I decided that once I complete my Chaplain course, I would like to get on the Pastoral Care Department's per diem roster where I would get called to be Chaplain when the need arises, though opportunities may be few and far between.

I briefly entertained the thought of going back to school and enrolling in a local university's Masters of Divinity program. I just want to take one class and see if I liked it. My peers, some of whom had graduated from that seminary, told me there was a Pastoral Care course. I thought about taking that to start.

I quickly put this idea out of my head. At the time I was 44 years old. I don't want to put my age as a factor because many people much older than I embark on new learnings. With working part time, I could only do a degree part time and I calculated that it would take eight years to achieve, putting me at age 52. I never intended on leaving the hospital so, once I had my degree, what would I do with it? The positive: I like learning and writing papers. The negative: I don't like to study. Master's degree was out.

My Chaplain internship was coming to an end. I wanted to keep my Chaplaincy going somehow but I just didn't know what to do.

Then, something happened in the Pastoral Care office. The office had a secretary whom I briefly had interactions with whenever I was in the office. Sometimes I would look at her and wonder to myself what her job must like. Everyone in the office was just so warm and understanding. I wondered what it would be like to really belong there.

Three months before the end of the Chaplain program, the secretary quit, and her position became vacant. Discernment stared me in the face once again. I thought about applying but weighed in so many factors. I had been in the ER, at this point, for over eight years and E.R. registration work was all I knew. I worked part time. I like having days off during the week and freedom of going places without crowds as most people were at work. I hadn't worked full time for 10 years and wondered if I'd be able to do it.

Ultimately, the deciding factor was my husband. One day I began to tell him about the open position and whether or not I should apply. He immediately said do it! That was all the affirmation I needed to hear. I went online and applied to be secretary of the Pastoral Care department.

APARA MAHAL SYLVESTER

15 DAY OF RECKONING

In the blink of an eye nearly eight months had passed since I embarked on my Chaplain intern journey. As part of my coursework, I had to write a final evaluation of myself using some guiding questions. This was part of my final evaluation from April 2018:

Explore my own pastoral authority (inadequacy) and issues related to it.

As the Chaplain program progressed, I became more confident in my Chaplaincy. I used to compare myself with other Chaplains whom I thought were better than me, but I stopped doing that. When I stopped comparing, I found my own "self," my own individual presence over time. I also used to second guess my actions and what I said, but I stopped doing that as well. In the end I can say that I was a good Chaplain. I served well and did the best that I could. I embraced my individuality, and this made me become a better Chaplain.

What were new things you learned about yourself over the course of this unit?

My resiliency and my presence. Initially I had issues of "letting go" of situations I encountered in the hospital and I felt the need to talk about them. I was frustrated when people (my family and others) didn't ask about how my on-calls or patient visits went. Over time, without even realizing it, I let this go. I was able to leave events and situations at the hospital without having the need to talk about them at home or with others. I think, in a way, by talking with others I was looking for validation of my actions. Slowly, the need for validation dissipated. I became my own validator.

Describe one aspect of your theology or beliefs that you examined and was challenged, changed, or affirmed.

Belief in the afterlife. I was always a strong believer in the afterlife, in heaven. My belief was affirmed in an encounter with a dying patient who asked me what I believed the after-life to be. I told him I believed in a heaven, and he affirmed my answer. In seeing sickness, dying, and suffering I cannot believe that this is all in vain, that there is not a better place that we all go to in the end. So, my belief in the afterlife has been affirmed.

What have you discovered about your strengths and growing edges?

In a previous evaluation I listed patience as my strength and confidence as my growing edge. I still believe that patience is my strength. I can listen to patients and family without getting fidgety. I can listen to and absorb what they say slowly and clearly. I can remain in a situation until I am no longer required, however long it takes. My growing edge, confidence, has changed quite a bit. I have become more confident in my role as Chaplain, and I no longer second guess what I do. This change occurred when I stopped comparing myself to others and embraced my individual self. It became a liberating feeling to just be me and to know that I am doing the right thing, what I am supposed to do.

APARA MAHAL SYLVESTER

16 KINGDOM OF HEAVEN

Nine months passed by in the blink of an eye. Before I knew it, May 2018 had arrived. I graduated from the Chaplain program and I was hired to be Secretary of the Pastoral Care department.

I was in Heaven.

In an Email to a friend I wrote:

After months of prayer, hope, and faith, I got offered the position of Secretary, Pastoral Care department. My start date will be June 11th. My last day in the ER will be Thursday May 31st. I will go from working part time evenings and holidays to a regular old 8:30 a.m.-5 p.m. job with no weekends or holiday requirements.

It will be quite a transition, but one I welcome with open arms. I love the Pastoral Care department, and I can't wait to be a permanent part of it.

On top of that, I met the CPE requirement of 300 clinical and on-call hours as Chaplain. Well, I actually did 300.65 hours, to be exact. 300.65 hours of doubt, insecurity, uncertainty, second-guessing, patience, confidence, faith, peace. I experienced death, suffering, life, joy, pain, and acceptance. Nine months later, I just don't know where the time went. In the end, I did the best that I could, and I'm proud of what I did.

I was Secretary of the department for two years until I got promoted to department Office Coordinator. In my role, all of my clerical and administrative skills from years past were utilized. Nothing went to waste. As I had once developed a prayer "toolkit," I also developed an administrative one which allowed the office operations to run smoothly under my care.

Prayer is still a big part of me. We have a morning report where the on-call Chaplain briefs others on the cases of the previous night. Afterwards we "pray in" the day. Once in a while, I offer to pray. Not often, as I still worry that I may stumble with my words. No matter how much we practice, I guess we can't be a perfectionist in everything. That's okay.

There's a security guard who I've known ever since I started working for the hospital. When he used to see me in

my Chaplain "hat" he would always say "Pray for me."
My faithful response was "Always." Now, some years later,
our dialogue has evolved a bit. When I pass him in the hallway he'll say "Yes?" and I'll respond "Yes!" meaning that he
still wants prayer and that I still pray for him. To this day I still
keep him in my prayers.

I have a great deal of contact with incoming CPE student
interns with similar anxieties and doubts as I once had. To
them I can say I understand. I did it too. It will be okay.
You'll love it! I'm happy to answer their questions about
CPE and maybe ease their nerves just a little.

All of us in the office share a common bond: We all have
experienced sickness, grief, death, and dying. Though I'm not
a Chaplain anymore, in many ways I still provide ESS.
Many times, I'll provide a listening ear to the Chaplains when
they've had a tough case and want to talk. I haven't been
exactly in their shoes to understand as no case is the same, but,
thanks to my training and experience, I do have a level of
understanding.

In order to view our paystub, we access the Employee Self
Service portal, which is abbreviated to ESS. The login button
says ESS Sign In. I always smile when I see this. Wouldn't it
be great if, when we needed it, we could simply click a button
and access ESS on-demand which, in my mind will always be
emotional and spiritual support.

I am beyond blessed to be working with a group of Chaplains who provide ESS on a daily basis to patients, families,
and staff.

Sometimes Chaplains debate over who will carry the pager. Many times, I'm tempted to jump in and offer myself, but that's not my role anymore. I always loved being on call with that pager, waiting for it to go off or not. I guess the "adrenaline junkie" that was in me never left.

My plan is to retire from this position. Well, this is my plan. I do hope and pray God has the same intent in mind. I've found a home in the Pastoral Care office and home is where I want to be.

Once in a while a Chaplain will tell me "I'm so happy that you're here." My response is always "I'm happy to be here." I am. Every day and counting.

Slowly but surely, I became what I was meant to be. I found my calling. I'm doing God's work in Chaplaincy, which is why I used God so often in my chapter headings whenever Chaplaincy came up.

I found my calling. If you look deep inside, you'll find yours, too. I know it's there.

The End

Made in the USA
Middletown, DE
25 August 2021